DISCONNECT TO CONNECT

How to Be Liked, Get Hired and
Make Your Family Proud... Offline.

By Betsy Jean Ricketts

Penhall Publishing
San Diego, California
www.penhallpublishing.com

ISBN 978-0-9897893-8-7 Paperback
978-0-9897893-9-4 Electronic Book Text

Library of Congress Control Number: 2020908016

Edited by Cynthia Gregory
Cover and interior design by Lilly Penhall
Interstellar Graphics
Cover images courtesy of Shutterstock

DEDICATION PAGE

To my parents and their parents, to my best friend and husband, our sons and daughter, to my sister, my godparents, my godson, my entire family, my dear old and new gal pals, especially to my CSU C3 girlfriends, and to all the people in my little world that I've learned from, loved and experienced life with... thank you.

More Praise for Betsy Jean Ricketts

"In *Disconnect To Connect*, Betsy shares her not only expert advice, but heartwarming stories and personal reflections from life on the road as a successful executive. Never missing an opportunity to engage with others, her experiences can help re-shape and enrich our experiences at home, work, and in-between. A must read for all professionals in the digital era."

– Anna Ford, Founder and CEO of Bookclubz

"Betsy gives us a much needed nudge and reminder of the importance of giving each other the place to connect in person and really *see* each other."

– Lorne Rubis, *The Character Triangle: Build Character, Have an Impact and Inspire Others*

"If I were to sit down and write a book about kindness and what it means to be a good human in the digital age, this would be it. Betsy has taken special care to present us with a treasure that can be enjoyed in a single sitting, or enjoyed and applied in parts. Thank you for this reminder that as technology and social norms may change, the values of kindness and personal accountability will always be timeless."

– Chris Kurtz, Chief Kindness Officer, Do Good. Be Kind.®

4

TABLE OF CONTENTS

I LIKE PEOPLE

Like many people I have met, loved or lost, I have succeeded and I have fallen. I have learned the hard lessons of burning a bridge and the sheer power of words to accidently help, hurt or heal my friends, colleagues and strangers throughout my entire life. I am in the people business. I also make it my business to frankly give a shit to all those that surround me, bump into me, or must work with me.

We as a society and human race have dramatically lost touch with our surroundings and each other and how life can and should be lived—eye to eye.

We have truly become addicted to a screen to make ourselves busy, occupied, emotionally charged and excused from interacting with others in business, in our community and with our family and friends. Our eyes have been glazed over by technology and now it is time to lift our heads up. We need to start living our lives (again) offline and in the real world.

You never know who you are going to

connect with, help or be helped by, with just starting to say "hi" to a stranger. We have so much to lose if we don't and so much to gain if we do.

So... eyes up, phone down, ears on and let's start with a hello.

MY WISH FOR YOU

My wish for you as you read this book, is to be open to the life you are living right now and enjoy the experiences you are creating, the people who are in your life who can support you, love you and who can learn from you.

I have slowly learned to appreciate the spontaneity, the circumstance, and the chances in life that enabled me to connect with new and old friends, as well as strangers. I am aware now that they can become staples in my life of enjoyment, challenge, laughter, and kinship and in turn empower me to live a life I fully enjoy.

I wish that you can relate to the lessons I went through where I learned to engage with others better.

I wish that a new friendship for you is born, such as a bond is made at work, at school or in your community and activities, as well as in your love life, friend life and family life.

I wish that you help someone in need,

and that you are recognized for being a good person—a person that cheers another on to meet their goal and in turn, you can experience the power of helping a person rise.

I wish that making a choice to disconnect from a device, an app or videogame for a short time or a day or even a month will give you back valuable time to live your life with the people that are in it—and in turn for you to receive joy, contentment, deeper growth and success.

"Deep human connection is...the purpose and the result of a meaningful life—and it will inspire the most amazing acts of love, generosity, and humanity."

– Melinda Gates

MY FRIEND EMILE

We never know what type of great person we can learn from by just raising our hand and being willing to talk to a stranger. That's how I met my friend Emile.

Everything happens for a reason. This is true even in a seemingly inconsequential event such as walking outside Charlie Palmer's near the U.S. Capitol after a lunch meeting and hailing a cab to go to my hotel. I am so happy I picked up your cab, Emile. After 10 minutes of a nice conversation you offered (on a wish) to take me further to the airport as the traffic was bad and I needed to get there quickly. I certainly appreciated your thoughtfulness.

I enjoyed hearing your stories of genuine and generous people you have had as customers. I appreciated you letting me share with you all about my work. I appreciated the connection you and I made about family. I shared with you a very scary day years ago in May where my husband and I almost lost everything in childbirth, which we all now mark as a happy day of our survival. It turns out—it was also the same day as your birthday where you were hoping to celebrate with your adult son visiting for the weekend. During our time together, I became more curious about your great attitude on life and your joy of meeting strangers, like me. I loved that our conversation ended with confessions to each other that we both wanted to write a book someday.

Thank you, Emile, for your friendship that day and as it continues over the years to come. I am excited to cheer you and your family on from across the country.

FOREWORD

I am grateful for my new friendship with Ms. Betsy, and I am humbled and honored to be asked to provide my advice on the value of engaging people in our lives.

1. Never look down on any one person in life, the least of them, may surprise you and have the best story for you.

2. Try to be as tolerant and open minded as much as you can, for the sky is limitless.

3. Humility and steadfastness are wonderful character traits, for one to inculcate.

4. It is not only as to how one sees themselves, but more importantly, as to how others see you.

5. There is no greater wealth in this world of ours than peace of mind.

6. As human beings, we all have days where we feel we can't survive. Sometimes dreams are shattered, friendships fall apart, loved ones may hurt us, sickness may overtake us, but GOD will always be there to guide us through, even during the toughest

of times.

7. Always be thankful for your life, as difficult as it may be. Wake up every day and be grateful. Everything you need as an individual for your destiny and internal glory is within reach.

8. One of the most important attributes for one to have, in the process of engaging people in our lives, is to be kind and gentle. Always try to see situations and things from other people's perspectives with the "glass half-full and half empty syndrome." Taking the dirt off your own eye, before telling someone else about the dirt in their eye.

9. We should stop pre-judging others... "judge not that you may be judged." Give others the benefit of the doubt, until they prove not worthy of the respect and dignity you bestowed upon them.

10. Finally, my most important attribute of engaging people is to show empathy. It's because it shows your level of concern for the person's wellbeing. Put yourself in another person's shoes. This helps us as individuals to be more relatable; it helps us to know how others feel, and how to respond accordingly

to their concerns.

Emile Ashwood is a graduate of Strayer University with a Masters of Education, is a former public school teacher and is currently a cab driver in the District of Columbia. Emile is from Sierra Leonne and has been in the U.S. since 1982. Emile and his wife, a graduate of Howard University, reside in Maryland with their son.

Betsy and Emile,

May 2019

WHY?

"Connection. The energy that exists between people when they feel seen, heard, and valued; when they can give and receive without judgment; and when they drive sustenance and strength from the relationship."

– Brené Brown

CHARACTER

What kind of a person are we? My Grandpa Jack would say about someone he respected... "He is a good man." That was it. What this meant is that my Grandpa Jack appreciated and valued the man's contributions, enjoyed interacting with him, and likely believed the man deserved good things.

As humans, we have both good and bad characteristics or tendencies or habits or a mindset that dictates how we act. But that doesn't mean we are simply good or bad people.

The description of character is "the mental and moral qualities distinctive to an individual," like what makes our personality, our temperament or combination of qualities that we can see and makes us different.

Growing up in my family, I learned what both my grandparents did for a living, like teaching, military service, coaching and being small business owners. I learned that their quality of life and particularly their success was built on providing service to others and being entrusted to take care of others and their children.

There are big responsibilities for any of us in this life as we are trusted to do the right thing, make the right decisions and do right by others.

We must be respected by others to obtain employment, build a business or be trusted by others with their possessions, their children or their livelihood.

We also have so much power to engage and make fulfilling relationships—simply by deciding to have a positive, hopeful and open attitude to any possibility.

"A good character is the best tombstone; those who love you and were helped by you will remember you when forgets me not have withered. Carve your name on hearts, not marble."

– Charles H. Spurgeon

TRUST, LOVE, RESPECT

In my journey as a professional businesswoman and in part of inheriting a wonderful family legacy—I believe the three biggest and most important characteristics of making up my own character are trust, love and respect.

Trust: Assumed reliance on the character, ability, strength or trust of someone and in which confidence is placed.

Love: An intense feeling of deep affection for another in a range of strong and positive, emotional and mental states; from the deepest interpersonal affection to the simplest pleasure.

Respect: Feeling of deep admiration for someone elicited by their abilities, qualities or achievements.

In this life, we must rely on others to not only accomplish our own goals but to simply assist us in conducting our life. This includes being born, being fed and clothed, being taught and hired, falling in love, finding a pet or birthing a child, and finally on our death bed. Most importantly we need each other to have the opportunity to love and be loved, to earn trust and be provided respect.

Give yourself the opportunity to do right by others and feel good at the end of your day or at the end of your life.

> "Reputation is what men and women think of us; character is what God and angels know of us."
>
> – Thomas Paine

REPUTATION BUILDERS AND KILLERS

Number One. Be Honest.

Communicating honestly can be a challenge. If you choose to be dishonest, you will lose being trusted and respected by others, and in turn by those who learn of this for the rest of your life.

Number Two. Be Truthful.

Telling the truth is an easy thing to do and the best way to defend any action or decision you ever make. A lie can be easier to do but can never be taken back or amended. Ever. The lie also easily builds where you can't go back, it's remembered forever and of course, can harm your reputation forever.

Number Three. Keep a Promise.

Your word, your handshake, your agreement with another is the power you have been given to build and maintain your reputation. Being trusted with the promise and following through is an example of a life well lived. Breaking a promise for any reason is a break in your reputation that has terrible ripple effects on your relationships, your career and to your character.

Number Four. Work Hard.

Do your job well, whatever it is, for whatever reason you have, for whatever time you are there. Doing your best is a great characteristic and speaks well of you. When no one is looking, work harder because you never know when someone is watching and it can change your circumstance, forever.

You can easily earn the respect of your boss, colleagues and family by doing a job well. All of them will take offense and discount your abilities if you portray laziness, are disenfranchised or are not dependable.

Number Five. Stand Up.

Show allegiance to your beliefs, to your boss and to your friends. Be someone who has another person's back, a person who deserves your respect and has morals and beliefs that are worthy of representing and standing up for. The risk of standing down is that you are denying your right to have your voice heard, your beliefs known, and your allegiance recognized.

Number Six. Be Present.

Be engaged in the moment where you are at any time of your life, your circumstance, your now. Exhibit your desire to be involved, dedicated and committed to what you are doing, who you are with and what experience you are having at the time. Otherwise, others can instantly discount your presence if you are unfocused, uncommitted or unattached to them or your situation.

Number Seven. Be Sincere.

When you show you care, when you genuinely express your thoughts or feelings, you earn the trust and respect of others. Trying to be charming instead is only for self-interest and will quickly be perceived as a fake sentiment.

Number Eight. Be Anonymous.

When you do something good and are satisfied with yourself and with your decision, you may truly not need or desire recognition for it. Only then are others more inclined to give you more praise and admiration solely based on your intent of not needing praise. When you decide to be recognized based on a desire to attract attention, your effort is self-serving and defeats the result.

Number Nine. Be Principled.

When you act with integrity and fairness, you know what is right and can exhibit those principles. A person earns respect and trust when they can be counted on as an ethical person who keeps themselves accountable and can be relied on to do right by others.

Number Ten. Be Strong.

When you have fortitude, you can better face adversity in any decision or situation. Being strong is to not take things personally but to stand by your convictions. You build honor instead of being weak minded or without purpose.

"There's nothing weak about kindness and compassion. There's nothing weak about looking out for one another. There's nothing weak about being honorable."

– President Barack Obama

JUST THAT ONCE

Always assume that if you do something one time only without better judgment, that someone will know or find out sometime, somewhere in the future.

A truly soul and reputation crushing statement… "It just happened that one time."

Always believe that when someone sees you or hears about it later, they will assume you always do that. If you go to work late on a Tuesday afternoon due to an important appointment regardless of the excuse, and you were late, they can assume you are always late to work.

Social media creates an instant exposure to whatever you say, do, feel, or the company you keep in any second.

Remember before you push the button or say something you might regret, you never know the audience or what the unintended consequences could mean for you, your family or your future.

> "All human actions have one or more of these seven causes...chance, nature, compulsions, habit, reason, passion, desire."
>
> – Aristotle

YOU ARE NOT ALONE

We all sometimes feel lonely, separate from others, and not connected. It's important to recognize that all others are experiencing life's up and downs, too.

Regardless of what a person looks like or what you assume he/she has or doesn't have, reach out and let someone know you support them on whatever journey they are in. The effort enables both of you to make a connection and may help them feel less lonely.

So many factors keep us fragmented from each other physically, which can include our schedules, our lives, our commute, our jobs, and our social environment.

Find opportunities to make a connection with anyone that shares that part of our daily or weekly journey whether it's a fellow colleague, commuter, coffee shop customer, security worker, bus driver, gym rat, bar buddy, or church friend.

> "Communication—the human connection—is the key to personal and career success."
>
> – Paul J. Meyer

EYEBALL TO EYEBALL

We have limited our opportunities for personal interaction. For those who are shy or uncomfortable around people, they have found other avenues to speak to people through a buffer. Video games, social media, voice and direct messages and texts are the first options to engage. Talking to people without really talking and not seeing them in person is not what life is about.

Human interaction can be exciting, fulfilling, reassuring and caring. In addition, expressing a compliment or showing empathy is important to being joyful in life.

YOU NEVER KNOW

You never know who you are going to connect with, help, or be helped by. You can start by just saying "hi" to a stranger.

There is so much to gain and so much to lose if we don't.

We need to start engaging as a society, as the human race has dramatically lost touch with our surroundings and how life can and should be lived with each other.

We have truly become addicted to our screens in order to feel busy and to find enjoyment from life. There is a cost to this approach and it's time for us to grab back our ability to connect—authentically, wholeheartedly, and without a device to support us.

"When there is no human connection, there is no compassion. Without compassion, then community, commitment, loving-kindness, human understanding, and peace all shrivel. Individuals become isolated, the isolated turn cruel, and the tragic hovers in the forms of domestic and civil violence."

– Susan Vreeland

WHAT?

"What we remember, what we treasure in the end, are the spontaneous, intimate moments when we feel connected with a beloved human being."

– Peggy O'Mara

WHAT NICE IS

We can all identify qualities of what being nice is... but in the context of connecting with others, consider nice as:

1. Fair.
2. Agreeable.
3. Engaging.
4. Approachable.
5. Engaging.
6. Thoughtful.
7. Caring.
8. Appropriate.
9. Enjoyable.
10. Respectable.

"If only you could sense how important you are to the lives of those you meet; how important you can be to people you may never even dream of. There is something of yourself that you leave at every meeting with another person."

– Fred Rogers

WHAT NICE IS NOT...AND WHEN TO KNOW THE DIFFERENCE

Anyone who works in design can tell you that what inhabits a space is as important as what does not. Nice is like that, too. Here is a short list of what nice is *not*.

1. Too Nice.

Being too nice is a negative quality or is at the very least questionable behavior because it seems you are trying to please everyone and being too emotional.

2. Indecisive.

When you can't make a decision or when you don't want to hurt other people's feelings regardless of what the best result should be for everyone's benefit.

3. Ineffective.

Can't we all get along? In a business environment you need to be productive and efficient; being incapable of performing your responsibilities does not make you an effective employee who supports the company's mission.

4. Evasive.

When you can't be direct and honest or avoid the need to give feedback it won't be taken well; don't expect to be taken seriously.

5. Indifferent.

"They're nice... but." If you've said these words before, don't think you're fooling anyone. Just that word "but" in this context is negative. It means that you have nothing else to contribute, are being blah, or simply indifferent.

6. Stuck or Immobile.

If you can't decide, can't be flexible or can't decide to be kind? Not good.

7. Settling for Less Respected.

It's not a good adjective for the business world. It can mean soft or not strong enough to do the job.

8. Being Spineless.

Spineless may mean you won't be mean or vindictive, so you won't likely cause harm to others around you. That's good, but you do have to stand up for yourself, have a backbone and call someone out respectfully when you need to.

9. A People Pleaser.

You don't have to please everyone. But being too accommodating or changing your ideals to not offend anyone doesn't work... and may count against you in the end.

10. Being Afraid to Say No.

You are entitled to your opinion. You can be consistent with your needs or your ideals by kindly saying no with conviction.

WHAT DO YOU SAY... TO BE NICE?

Sometimes a kind word is the very best thing you can offer the world and the people you care about. Try one of these:

1. Cheers! Woo Hoo! Bravo! Hooray! Congratulations!

2. Atta Boy or Atta Girl!

3. Bless Your Heart. (the sincere version)

4. Good for You.

5. Wish You the Best.

6. Way to Go!

7. Best Wishes.

8. You Can Do It.

9. Go Get Em!

10. You Are a Rockstar!

WHAT DO YOU SAY... TO SHOW EMPATHY?

Empathy: the action of being aware of, being sensitive to, and vicariously experiencing the feelings, thoughts and experiences of another without having the feelings, thoughts, and experiences fully communicated in an explicit manner.

Sharing empathy shows that you know what it is to be a caring, compassionate human. If you're new at this type of behavior, try one of these:

1. It's Going to Be Okay.
2. I Hear You.
3. You Can Do It.
4. I'm Proud of You.
5. I Think You are Amazing.
6. I'm Excited for You.
7. I'm Concerned About You.
8. How Can I Help?
9. Are You Doing Okay?
10. I Wish I Could Make It Go Away.

> "The great gift of human beings is that we have the power of empathy. We can all sense a mysterious connection to each other."
>
> – Meryl Streep

WHAT DO YOU SAY...
TO SHOW SYMPATHY?

Sympathy: Feelings of pity and sorrow, compassion, understanding and reaction to the distress of others.

We've all been there, and sometimes we were on the receiving end when we really needed it. It takes so little effort and pays such rich dividends!

1. I Am Thinking of You.

2. Wishing You Peace.

3. My Deepest Condolences.

4. With My Sympathy.

5. I'm Sorry for Your Loss.

6. This Must Be So Hard for You.

7. I Hope You Can Find Comfort During This Difficult Time.

8. I Hope You Can Be Surrounded by Strength and Compassion.

9. My Heart Goes Out to You.

10. Please Remember That I Love and

Care About You and Will be Here
for You Always.

"There simply is no pill that can replace human
connection. There is no pharmacy that can fill the need
for compassionate interaction with others."

– Dr. Joanne Cacciatore

HOW?

"Human connection is the most vital aspect of our existence, without the sweet touch of another being we are lonely stars in an empty space waiting to shine gloriously."

– Joe Straynge

HOW TO BE A PEOPLE PERSON

Being the kind of person who cares for others is not a big mystery. You must be alive, you have to care, and you have to be engaged.

1. Give a Sh*t.

Be interested about what you do and what and who you care about. Be invested in what happens. Be caring to others and generally cheer others on. Be compassionate about something. Be concerned about what is happening in your world and how it impacts others you care about.

2. Pay Attention.

Be engaged in your environment and recognize what is happening around you. Look around, understand your surroundings, and learn about what others are deciding that can impact you. When in any environment, keep your head up and eyes and ears open to others.

3. Be Genuine.

Be your true self, don't hide who you are or what you care about. When you tell someone something, mean it. Truly. When you say thank you, be sincerely thankful and make sure that they feel appreciated and know you are real.

4. Walk Out the Door.

Choose to be open to experiences. Get out of the house, the office, the city you are in and do something different. Learn or try an experience you want or be open to try something new. Pick an activity and then immerse yourself in another world to give you perspective and joy.

5. Reach Out.

Say hello. Make an excuse to reach out and connect with someone. Take the initiative and make the first move. You can also take an approach to start the connection in order to keep the relationship and create the opportunity for both of you to get something out of the contact.

6. Be Curious.

Be interested in someone's interest, in

something new, in anything that piques your own interest. Be thirsty for insight, information, perspective, knowledge and joy.

7. Remember the Good Stuff.

Don't hold a grudge by remembering the poor decisions of others. Be someone others appreciate when you remember them from a previous connection that was good. More importantly, remember what is important to them and their perspective of life. This will be a game changer.

8. Do it for Free.

Offer something for nothing in return. Be helpful to another for the sole purpose to support another person because you can and it's what they need. Ask if someone needs assistance, offer anything sincerely and be ready to give, and be thoughtful of what should be given for their highest good.

9. Be Generous.

Be giving of your time, of your attention and of a resource that is worth sharing with another.

10. Be Happy for Them.

Be sincere when congratulating someone,

wishing them the best, and being honest when you tell them, "I'm happy for you." Truly mean what you say. Your words and the conviction you put behind those words matter and can be felt. People connect the best with you when they receive genuine interest and support from others; if you are happy for them, they will be happier for themselves.

BE A GOOD SPORT

No one likes a poor sport. It means the world to someone when a winner (or a loser) has the grace to say, "well done." It's not so hard... if you practice these methods:

1. Be Loyal.

Be a diehard loyal fan of your family, of your friends, of your passion, and your craft.

2. Cheer Them On.

Support your own team, let them know you know it can be done. Recognize everyone's engagement and cheer on the fight, your teammate's tenacity and their future victory.

3. Listen to Coach.

Find a mentor, learn from your boss, your parent or a colleague. Seek someone out who especially wants you to succeed to be a better person and win in life.

4. First Pitch.

You must start somewhere. You have to show up at the plate, be a part of the game, give yourself a chance and be in it to help your team succeed.

5. After the Buzzer.

Do not stop until the very end. Don't assume you won, don't slow down, or be presumptuous. Don't be a poor winner when you might lose in the end. Assume you can still win and still be victorious until the very last one-hundredth of a second.

6. Good Job, Good Job.

Shake hands at the end with your opponent. Thank them for giving their all as it challenged you both to fight hard and understand that the race was worth it to you both. You never know when you'll see them next or how you both may possibly reconnect.

7. Take a Knee.

A game stops being a game the very second someone gets hurt. Take a moment, recognize the person with an injury, pray and encourage them regardless of the circumstance, whether they are friend or foe. It could have been you. You never know when it's your last play, so send them all the energy you can that everyone can stand and clap when they hopefully walk off the field.

8. Put Me in Coach.

Be a team player. Help your team anyway you can. Be ready to play and give it your all. Have the confidence to know that you are here for a reason, that you can perform, and you will give it your all to achieve an ideal state to the benefit of yourself—and others.

9. Brush it Off.

Get back up. Do it again because you can, you should, and you will feel great when you do. Turn off the noise, focus on your intent, the job, and your follow through. It's going to be okay, it's just a minor setback and roadblock to test you and make the finish line truly worth it when you finally cross it. Those who can stand back up after falling have a superpower. Keep going.

10. Celebrate Good Times.

Celebrate the start of the season, celebrate the opportunity of getting in the game, and celebrate the end of the season with a bit of reflection and nostalgia. Celebrate the hard-won victories, the ability to keep going, your teammates' accomplishments and your dedication, commitment and tenacity. At the end of the game, it will be important that you had fun.

REASONS TO REACH OUT TO A HUMAN

We live in a digital world. But seriously, there's so much more to a life being lived offline. Here is how you can be more human with others:

1.   Hi. Hello and How Are You?

2. Happy, Happy, Happy <u>(fill in the blank)</u>!

3. Congratulations.

4. I Hope all is Well.

5. Thinking of You.

6. I Am in the Neighborhood.

7. Someone Recommended You or Thinks Highly of You, and Suggested I Reach Out.

8. Do You Want My Help?

9. I Have Someone for You to Meet.

10. Can I Get Your Advice?

NOW WHAT

Once you make "hello" the beginning of a connection, how can you build something with them or see where it goes? Try these time-tested tips:

1. Introduce Yourself.

Share something about yourself once or twice.

2. Ask a Question.

Be curious. Are they coming or going? What do they care about? What is the purpose of why they are there? Pick up what they are saying and ask a follow-up question... "You mentioned you have a PhD... in what?"

3. Share Your World.

Be brave. Give a tidbit into who you are, what you do, or what your opinion of current state is.

4. What is a Common Bond?

Try to figure out what you have in common, or what they know that can be helpful to you.

5. Their Expert Opinion.

What can you learn from them? Ask another question. "What do you do? Tell me more."

6. Remember Their Name.

Repeat their name in conversation so you can better remember their name, make a connection with their name and what you have learned about them. Think about someone else you know with that name so when you look at your new connection you will remember their name better. This will help your memory because the name is familiar to you and you have an image in your head of their "namesake".

7. Offer Something.

How can you be helpful? What is my expertise or background that I can share my perspective? Is there someone or something you know that can be helpful to them in life or work?

8. Be Sincere.

Appreciate the time with them by telling them you enjoyed meeting them and share with them that you are interested in keeping in touch.

9. Leave a Paper Trail.

Create an opportunity or reason to stay in touch and provide your information or offer your business card.

10. A Real Goodbye.

Use eye contact and keep it real so they appreciate the contact and wish them well. Say the words and mean it.

THE "NO RULES" OF INITIAL CONTACT

Relationships are important. Strategic relationships are tricky. Here are some insider tips that may just help you pave the road to better relationships.

1. No Tissues.

Building a connection or relationship is important. It's a fine balance of being somewhat emotional with a bit of compassion, empathy and sharing a feeling. What isn't appropriate is an extreme display of emotion, oversharing or a burst of water works crying worthy of a box of tissues.

2. No Medals.

Sharing a success, or a great moment in your life with a new contact is acceptable but boasting excessively will not be well received. Don't expect a standing ovation for telling someone of an accomplishment.

3. No Novels.

Offering a perspective or a snippet of an

important part of your life is a great way to make a personal connection. However, no one wants to spend more than 3-5 minutes hearing a long story that they have no investment in and can't relate to. The extended version or novel of your life will do nothing but create a "bore and ignore" response from others.

4. No Needles.

When you are engaged in a connection and the other person is enthusiastic to share with you their news, revel in their happy time. Don't be pessimistic of their hope, don't ruin their surprise with a "Debbie Downer" comment or burst their bubble with a sarcastic or debilitating remark. There is no joy sharing good news with someone who has a bummer personality.

THE THANK YOU NOTE

Thank you—the strongest two words used together to start, build, make and keep a connection.

A stronger bond is developed when you

acknowledge a person's "gift" of anything of value and it is sincerely appreciated.

Being recognized positively for a good decision you make for others, and when you do it without reward, when you think no one is watching, should make you feel amazing.

I love the thought of receiving a thank you note, handwritten words in an envelope with the stamp and my name on it, like a diamond shining through the mail at work or home amongst all of the subscriptions, advertisements, bills and junk mail.

Buy a stamp, card and envelope, and then send a note to someone you want to know that you care and appreciate their effort. Your note can be about anything, big or small. It does not matter... just send it. Trust me, the recipient will feel your appreciation and is another great way to deepen your relationship.

SPEAK THE SAME LANGUAGE

When we communicate with fellow humans it's the best to speak each other's language.

There are a variety of ways to further improve communications with each other, language barriers notwithstanding.

Always try to communicate with your key person in the way that they communicate. Do they prefer text, LinkedIn message, email or a phone call? Do they prefer being contacted in the morning, lunchtime, evening or weekend? If your boss emails you with black Arial 12 font, reply in the same font as they will naturally be more receptive to your message because it's in their preferred "language" or context. Meet your fellow human where they are at.

HELLO OPERATOR

Use the phone. Talk to people with the phone, as it was designed to be used. Most importantly, show respect and remember their name.

I always try to call customer service and push 0. I ask for their help, show respect, listen for their name, and repeat their name back mid chat. I also try to create an opportunity for them to do the right thing, to do their job well and try to enjoy the 5 to 10 minutes (hopefully) that we must talk to each other. It's because neither of us want to be spending our time fighting each other over a bill, an order or an error.

Next time, take note of their name, remember it and use it. By repeating their name, it shows them you see them as a real human, and they will then be more helpful to you because you engaged with them positively. If you see them, it helps them to see you.

THE BODY IS THE ULTIMATE CONNECTOR

Brain.

Your voice, your conscious, and your curiosity connects the dots and people before you do.

Eyes.

Your vision notices everything, seeks something out, sends messages, identifies everything, and is the first thing to connect you to others.

Heart.

Your heart tells your brain what to do, provides compassion, enables love and the ability to feel good.

Arms.

Hugs are magic, holding hands provides reassurance, and a handshake enables goodwill and an agreeable connection.

HUMBLE PIE

Go ahead, eat it now. The sexiest and most adoring characteristic is being humble. Take a bite before you need it. Being humble is not convenient. It is innocent, necessary and oh so appreciated. No one deserves praise who thinks they automatically deserve it. More praise is given to those who are surprised, appreciative and thankful for the recognition. Be thankful and mean it. Be sincere and let it show.

THE THOUGHT THAT COUNTS

Think of a signature way to reach out to people to let them know who you are, to make another connection or continue engaging with them over the years in a unique way.

Not Your Normal Notecard.

I am more motivated to send a quick card

of hello, thanks, nice to meet you or thinking of you when the card I use is special and is only from me. In my 20s, I found little handmade cards of old-fashioned ladies with real feathers for hats and my name written on the bottom—unique, stylish and different like me. In my 30s, my wedding thank you notes, and professional correspondence cards were Cranes in blue and cream with my name on the top – simple and classic like me.

Pick a box (or 3) of stationery that you love, customize the cards to feel like you and be more encouraged to send something of you the old school way when making a connection.

Holiday Hellos.

How do you reach out to people you want to connect with? Every holiday I know my friend Jen will send me a personalized text with a seasonal greeting. I look forward to it and it's a way she can easily connect with me.

Pie Box.

Our good family friend bakes a pie for a friend or neighbor when they are sick or if they have suffered a loss in their family. Jerry has used the same white cardboard pie box for the last several decades, and the box is returned to him from the recipient when the pie has been enjoyed. There are a hundred signatures on the box of every single person who has received his love through pie. This is a beautiful and useful reminder of his gesture and for those who receive a pie know that they are not alone.

In a world where what we do is proof of who we are, let us all do good and be kind.

– Christopher Kurtz

WHERE?

"What most interests me is human connection, whether it's on the street, in community, through music, storytelling, and shared experience."

– Ben Sollee

AIRPORT TIPS AND RULES

1. Be Kind to Airport Staff.

The airport employees, airline staff and crew, and restaurant workers are there every day all day. They don't get out and are trapped with those of us who don't want to be there. We are forced to spend time in and around the terminal, and they are forced to provide us a service. Ask them how they are doing, appreciate their assistance, and look them in the eye when you thank them for their help.

2. Lips Up.

In the security line, walking the terminal, or waiting to board, look up and engage with those in your immediate area. Start a smile with edges of lips upturned, as to signal you are paying attention to them, that you acknowledge their presence and you are engaged in this shared experience with them. Start by showing a friendly face before flying the friendly skies.

3. Cruise the Concourse.

Take a walk all the way down the terminal and back. Check out the shops, pay attention to what cities you have a connection with that are on the monitors, and pay attention to the people around you and where they are flying to in effort to expand your horizons at least mentally.

4. Try Something New.

Be curious, be adventurous and pretend you are on a journey in a foreign land (only it's a new state to you within the United States). Everyone at the airport is from somewhere else or going somewhere else. Eat local, notice the variety of restaurants, look at menus for unique food from the area (i.e. "famous popcorn") and find a local gift for yourself and others.

5. Label Yourself.

One of the best ways to engage in conversations and find people in common is to wear something or have something that personalizes who you are, what you do, what you love or where you've been. Wear the logo of your college, your favorite sports team, a marathon shirt, or a baseball cap souvenir from your last trip. These can be used for positive conversation starters. "Did you go to school there?" "I love San Francisco too!" A great example is going through Midwest airports that are filled with field sales teams with their company shirts, which is great low-cost advertising and it's a unique way to learn about what they do or where they are from.

6. Read the Racks.

Learn something new about what other people are interested in. There are magazines for almost everyone's interests, and you would be surprised that some of them garner enough interest to warrant a monthly magazine readership. Go into the gift shop and make it a guilty pleasure to look through a few magazines that pique your interest and then buy one or two magazines that you are really interested in to learn more and explore a different point of view. Learn what others love or do in any magazine and identify what businesses or companies cater to those readers. What celebrities are pitching things? What didn't you know about science or health or the outdoors or travel or other nationalities? Treat the magazine rack as a pop culture pop quiz or an unrestricted Twitter feed.

7. Pay Attention.

When you see someone who catches your eye do you think: Do I know them? Do they look familiar? Who do they remind me of? Who do I know that I immediately think of who they could be connected to? It could be they caught your eye for a reason!

8. Getting on the Plane.

Look at the faces a few rows back and quickly scan others to see if you recognize them. Another opportunity is to scan first class to as they likely boarded before you may have seen them in the waiting area. Remember there are just six degrees of separation between strangers.

9. A Familiar or Friendly Face.

Scan the crowds and ask, "Do I know them?" or "Are they familiar?" or "Who is it I know that is connected to them?" Look at faces for you to remember later or for you to make a connection now for comfort. Once on the plane, befriend your seatmate with a smile.

10. Be Helpful.

Offer to help single parents that are alone with kids, sharing with them that you know exactly how they're feeling if you have kids of your own and you are happy to help. Immediately help others put up or take down their luggage, especially if they are physically limited from doing so. Be nice to the stewards and make their job easy to serve you as best they can.

ANYTIME AND EVERYWHERE

These time-tested guidelines apply pretty much to any situation you may find yourself in:

1. Be the Friendly Face in a Crowd.

Look up and recognize the person in front of you. Turn up your lips for a start of a smile. If you look approachable and open, you will be able to start a connection.

2. Say Hello.

The easiest way to connect with another is simply to acknowledge them and say hello. Sadly, more people than not are surprised and taken back to receive a nice "hi there" from a stranger and let their guard down.

3. Ask a Question.

Be curious, real and engaged. Ask someone how their day is going or their opinion on something in order to start a conversation.

4. Compliments are Free.

When you pay attention to someone else, to something they are doing or wearing, it will catch your attention and it gives you a great opportunity to seize the moment. When I see a woman wearing a beautiful jacket, I sincerely let her know that I love her jacket. Compliments go a very long way to build goodwill and confidence in others.

5. Be Kind.

Open a door, ask if someone needs help, be considerate of others in front of you and do something nice. Use kind words to another human and show a bit of compassion in any first interaction.

6. Offer to Help.

Recognize if someone needs help and make the decision to do something, large or small, to spontaneously be helpful.

7. You Never Know.

Let someone surprise you, in a good way. Building a connection now may help you in the future in ways that you may never know in the moment. Don't wait to find out that a bridge you didn't build, or burned, may have helped you in a tremendous way in the future. Are they your future roommate or boss, the potential love of your life or your child's future boss? You just never know.

8. Be Curious.

Go into a new shop or restaurant, buy a book in a bookstore, ask questions of those you meet. Try to learn something new from someone new.

9. Give Someone a Chance.

Say "yes" if someone offers to help and offer to do something helpful to someone new to you. Suspend your judgment for a moment to let yourself connect with someone you otherwise wouldn't.

10. Wish Them Well.

Be sincere in thanking them for their time to connect, and hoping they truly have a good day by saying it out loud.

MEETING MAGIC

Everyone has meetings for work or for volunteering. Team meetings, board meetings, staff meetings, budget meetings, sales meetings, trade association meetings, church meetings and nonprofit meetings. A meeting is to create the opportunity to build unity, communicate, inform and make decisions with a group of invited people for a specific time, a dedicated purpose and to meet a goal. Unfortunately, more technology can mean there are more meetings, more conference calls and virtual meetings. As a result, there is now less opportunity for people to connect with each other in person, to read body language and directly communicate without misconception.

How to pull out the magic in your

meetings:

1. Arrive Early.

Plan to arrive 5-10 minutes early to the meeting. However, don't arrive too early or the host will be put out. Find the bathroom and emergency exit, observe the room and take a few minutes to say hi to the host or initiate a quick chat with the speaker.

2. Check the Nametags.

Observe seating arrangements for the purpose of the meeting, help the host figure it out if it hasn't been figured out before. You can help determine where the most appropriate place is for everyone to sit down - including you. Do not rearrange tables or place cards for the sole benefit of yourself or to enable you to sit closer to the host or guest speaker.

3. Get Your Seat Ready.

Put your notepad, pen and business cards on the table, your phone on silent with "out of office" reply on and put your briefcase or purse under the table. Don't fidget or arrange your stuff while the host is trying to start the meeting.

4. Focus.

Focus on the purpose of the meeting, the goal for yourself to participate in the meeting, and determine the benefit or value of being in the meeting in the first place. Don't be disengaged or appear bored or preoccupied with your phone or texts or emails at any time during the meeting.

5. Participate.

Be engaged and attentive with the host. Continue holding eye contact with the speaker and remind them visually you are currently engaged and interested.

6. Listen First.

Listen to all the speakers with interest, write a few notes of what resonated the most, what you want to get out of it, and any action items for yourself after the meeting.

7. Talk Later.

Consider what one or two messages you believe you are the only one to have the unique perspective to share towards the end of the conversation. You can easily do this by adding to someone's comment or question.

8. Introduce Yourself.

Create opportunities for connecting with the attendees at the meeting to further help reach the goal.

9. Help Watch the Time.

The host will appreciate your support in watching the time, pointing to your watch with a comforting smile to the speaker indicating time is almost up, and indicate to others time is up by closing your notebook and putting the cap back on your pen.

10. Thank the Host with Feedback and Offer to Help.

Plan to spend a few minutes after the meeting touching base with the host, offer positive feedback, and use the opportunity to sign up for a task that came out of the meeting.

CONFERENCES

Professional conferences are a fabulous way to make new connections. Make the most of your time with one or a combination of the following:

1. Take a Look.

Review the agenda, the list of speakers you want to hear from, and how to make the most of the time you are dedicating to sharing a conference center with thousands of strangers.

2. Find the Connections.

Read the biographies of the speakers to find a possible connection with them. What are the topics and the speakers you want to learn more about?

3. Build Your Own Schedule.

Determine how best to spend your time on the priority meetings that will create opportunities for you to listen, learn and contribute to the conversations through one on ones after the sessions or asking the right question during the session.

4. Who's in the Crowd.

Ask for the attendee list before you arrive and review it before you get there. Review who will be with you as soon as you receive the list to identify who you may know, who you want to know and who may be connected to others you know.

5. Link Up Before.

Connect with the attendees you want to meet before the meeting. Create a short list of those you are wanting to see, find them on LinkedIn, send a message letting them know you will be there and that you are looking forward to seeing them at the meeting.

6. Be a Dinner Host.

Before you get to the meeting, reach out to a small group who you identify as people you would want to spend time with, who you want to connect others to, and who you know. Invite them all to a small dinner party after one of the receptions. Make the reservation for more guests than you have identified so you can invite more folks to join you after you make more new connections at the meeting. Find a place close to the hotel and invite others through email, text, or once you get there. When you arrive at the opening reception, find and remind your connections that you have organized a fun dinner and encourage them to join your group for dinner. Being a second host at the event and being inclusive to others is a great way to be known as a connector and will further help you make better connections while you are there.

7. Lobby Lounger.

Spend time around the registration desk of the hotel. Check into the meeting desk to see who has already arrived or who is still needing to pick up their nametag. Spend time in the common areas to be seen and to see others. Everyone needs to check-in so you will see everyone if you spot them in the lobby. Have a short list of people in mind who you want to see and look out for.

8. Bar Bums.

You will see people at the bar before, during and after the meeting. Plan to spend one drink (alcoholic or otherwise) in downtime with conference colleagues chatting and relaxing, but don't stay too long or too late which might negatively reflect on your reputation. Don't be seen by higher level execs or future business partners for spending too much time or money at the bar.

9. Be the Connector.

When you meet someone, figure out a way

to help others connect with someone else at the conference that will help them meet their goals or that you know has something they have in common.

10. The Note Ninja.

When you meet someone you truly want to engage with after the meeting, ask for their card with interest to connect. Make it the highest priority to follow up with them on the flight home or on the first day back to establish the connection and have them appreciate your engagement.

RESTAURANTS

Think of restaurants as more than a good meal and a chance to build connections. Make the most of your dining time with a few of these strategic tidbits:

1. Windows are for Looking Into.

When you are walking by a restaurant, look inside. Learn what's inside, who is there and what food is so good to make the place thrive. Looking through the glass may create a contact with someone you know who is only feet away from you. Glass should not prevent you from making a connection.

2. The Hostess is the Boss.

Be friendly to the host. Show appreciation of their restaurant, be patient to be seated and show respect to the person whose job is to make every guest and every waiter be glad they are there.

3. Be Curious.

Be willing to try the chef's specials and the restaurant's known dish. You can not only ask the waiter for their own recommendations but actually be willing to select one of them. Opening yourself to a new food experience broadens your perspective and is something to help you connect with others.

4. Table Mates.

Pay attention to the people around you. Congratulate the couple who is celebrating an anniversary, say hello to the grandma enjoying her 80th birthday with a second gin gimlet or ask your neighbor if they recommend you order the same thing they are enjoying. You never know how a conversation or relationship can start over a great meal wherever you are.

5. Potty Time.

Plan to go to the bathroom before the meal to wash your hands and again after the meal. You may not have a small bladder but creating the opportunity to walk through the dining room creates more exposure to the people around you coming and going while you are there.

6. Change the Path.

You may be escorted to your table one way but choose to leave the table another way to enable you to walk through another group of possible connections.

7. Bar Check.

Take a peek or walk through the bar. More people go in and out for a quick drink or bite so it's a good place to see and be seen.

8. Be Generous.

A part of a great dining experience is being able to show your appreciation with your waiter and chef with both a twenty percent plus tip and a compliment. Your generosity will be noticed by everyone around you when the staff is visibly happy you enjoyed the experience.

9. Ask a Local.

When in a new place, ask advice from someone who lives or works there. You can even ask your Uber driver or a shop owner what restaurant they recommend and what food to try—to get connected to the local scene.

10. Share the Secret.

When you find a gem of a place, or discover the best thing you ever ate, be gracious in sharing the name of the restaurant with someone you are connecting to with the hope that they enjoy the experience too.

WHO?

"Cherish your human connections—your relationships with friends and family."

– Former First Lady Barbara Bush

THE GREATEST PEOPLE EQUALIZERS

Sometimes it is hard to remember and easy to forget that we humans are more alike than we think. These are a few of the ways we are having a shared experience:

1. We want to be loved.

2. We all have 24 hours in a day.

3. We must wear clothes.

4. We all have to take bathroom breaks.

5. We must sleep somehow, somewhere and sometime.

6. We want to laugh, and we like it when we do.

7. We worry. A lot.

8. We know something or someone that brings us true joy.

9. We each have a "next Tuesday" trigger for whatever day is near. An anniversary, a death of a loved one, the big interview, the

big game, the deadline of the bill, and a birthday. Every date means something to someone.

10. We want to be recognized for doing good by anyone and anywhere.

"A tribe is a group of people connected to one another, connected to a leader, and connected to an idea. For millions of years, human beings have been part of one tribe or another. A group needs only two things to be a tribe: a shared interest and a way to communicate."

– Seth Godin

BONDS: WE ARE RELATED OR ALREADY CONNECTED

We may feel like the only person on the planet sometimes, but it just isn't true. Think of all the people you know and consider how many ways you are connected from the following list:

1. Immediate family

2. Extended family

3. School friends

4. College alumni or college roommate

5. School sweetheart

6. Neighborhood pal or 'we grew up together'

7. Current or former colleague

8. Boss or employee

9. Sport team fan or special interest member

10. Mutual friend

BONDS: WE HAVE A COMMON CONNECTION

When you meet a stranger try to find one thing that you have in common. It's not as hard as you may think. You may discover you share more than one of the following:

1. Current or former resident of the same state or town

2. Same industry

3. Same college

4. Fraternity brother or sorority sister

5. Same employer or former employer

6. Same animal lover

7. Same sports team fan

8. Same food lover

9. Favorite drink drinker

10. Same vacation spot visitor

OUR RESPONSIBILITY FOR CONNECTING OTHERS

When you successfully introduce two connections to benefit them both, you will then be seen with more respect, trust, appreciation and as a generous spirit.

There's a great opportunity and reward for introducing two people to each other. There is also a great risk and potential downfall for either person, or for yourself, if no one is happy with the results of the connection.

A good way to approach the introduction is to think of presenting someone in front of a CEO. You must decide which person you want to present the other person to who has something to give to the person who may have more power or respect. You are vouching for the person being introduced and you both need to show respect to the "CEO". Furthermore, the CEO should trust that you will not waste their time and that you believe the person you are introducing will be valuable and worth their while to meet.

When you introduce others to build a relationship, to hire someone, or meet up on a single date, they are absolutely going to be more grateful to be introduced and find value from you.

At the end of any day it's your reputation on the line and what you do and who you influence is a reflection on who you are and how you put your reputation to good use in order to help others.

MY LIFE INFLUENCERS

1. Grandma Madalyn.

She was bold, tough, had balls, worked very hard and enjoyed her life. She was not a people person, but she cared a lot about people. Gramma had the guts to sell their wedding gift of lambs while Grandpa was in the Navy. She made the bold decision for her new family to leave the family farm and instead buy a little motel in town with 10 cabins to give them a house to live in during the school year as they were teachers, and had a business to run during the summer months when their school was out. Gramma did everything well with intent. She taught me to treat every person well, to fold every bed corner the same way and to not take everything so seriously. While she never enjoyed receiving praise, she was proud being seen in the gymnasium for decades as a high school basketball coach and then a steadfast fan until the day she died. My Gramma should have been proud for what her family contributed to their small town.

2. Bob Fritz at Seattle Fudge.

Bob gave me my first big kid job in Seattle. I learned a lot about running a small business, about customer service - and a way to fuel my love of candy and sugar. I spent a summer in a little popcorn cart near the Space Needle eating my share of hot dogs or working summer festivals and dealing with melting fudge and sticky taffy. Bob encouraged me to study business in college instead of heading to culinary school, which was great advice for my career and yet I still got to take a baking class at a culinary school decades later.

3 and 4. Danny Tomlinson and Stan Sours.

Being a young woman lobbyist in my early 20s was at a unique time and the environment was challenging. But the power, long term relationships and money that helped influence some legislators (which I had none) were soon regulated with campaign-finance reform and term limits which let my foot in the door. Stan, Danny and a small group of reputable behind-the-scenes men of honor lobbyists taught me how to communicate with legislators and staff, how to learn the rules of the legislative process, earn respect and most importantly to be the first in the door and last one to leave the Capitol. They also taught me to be present, tell the truth and help find the answer.

5. Deb Tamlin and the Colorado REALTORS®

Deb was a strong tireless leader in every world she was entered. She was dedicated to the REALTOR® profession and became a long-standing leader in the political world for them. She knew her community, she knew her business, she knew the legislators and was restless and ready for a good fight on property rights whenever it was needed. Deb was one of the best volunteers of the trade association I worked for, as she was the one who wanted to learn more but could easily teach others at the same time. She also made late nights at the Capitol or stressful high-pressure legislative meetings bearable. We were at election night events together for years and Deb was great to call a friend and mentor. And I always remember a REALTOR® unwritten rule—have a business card at the ready... always.

6. Lydia Beebe.

Lydia was a quiet steadfast leader. She was a powerhouse executive who was caring and without ego. She was a mom and a lawyer and sat in the room of the Board of Directors of one of the most powerful energy companies for decades, which had to be so stressful as one of the few women in the room and paving the way for all of us. I assume it was ever challenging to want and need balance in her life being an hour away from her family and never having it impact her professional responsibilities. I'm proud of Lydia as an incredible class act and how she always conducted herself, even when she was not treated with the respect that she clearly should have been. Lydia deserved better but she's okay with that and for that I respect her even more. I greatly appreciated her advice, counsel and support (over a glass of champagne) as my professional advisor and supporting me to do what I need to do for both my career and family.

BRAND BACKPACK

Everyone has a connection with a brand. A favorite beer, city, sports team, clothing designer, animal or pet, activity, food or restaurant.

We also all have connections to our preferences, to our shared experiences, our religion or spirituality, or to organizations that mean something to who we are.

What if we knew each other through the brands we associate with? What if we could connect with others just by knowing what they love?

Without an opportunity for us to put all of our personal brand preferences on a backpack and wear it around for everyone one to see to help build connections, kinship and relationships - try to find a way to share the little or big things with others that bring you joy. What's on your brand backpack?

I would pick 10 "badges" to illustrate my brand preferences or things that are meaningful that I would put on a backpack to share with others, and another way for others to make a connection with me:

1. Pepsi.

Sundays with dad on the living room floor watching sports. I will always prefer Pepsi any day of the year.

2. Doritos.

My favorite snack for years in college. Cheese flavor, and nothing else compares. By the way, whatever happened to original Doritos?

3. Starbucks.

In high school in Seattle we stopped by

(the 3rd ever) Starbucks on our way to school every single day. I have great memories of tall nonfat mochas topped off with whip cream with by best girlfriends. If Starbucks wasn't going to go public by the time I graduated, my friend Erica and I had developed our own logo for an international coffee company. Nothing beats a hot coffee on a cold rainy day to make me happy.

4. Broncos.

Anytime I see a Broncos sticker or someone wearing a Bronco hat I smile, and it makes me happy. Only one year of the decade-plus living in Denver did I get to go to the games as a season ticket holder guest, but it was the finest year to be a part of a great group of fans and where so many of my friends and their family generations have enjoyed cheering on these great professional athletes.

5. Chi Omega.

The sorority to me was a great opportunity to feel a sense of belonging in college. I gained so many friendships and learned so much about leadership being part of the Chi Omega house. Having a small (or large)

97

group of friends in college means you have friends through your life you can count on—to support your job search, to be in your wedding, and later to be there for you when perhaps you suffer a terrible loss of a spouse, of a child or of a parent.

6. Walt Disney World.

I went with my family in 5th grade and then again my senior year of high school. I love anything "behind the scenes" and as a guest, I always wondered what was behind those "Cast Only" doors. After being given the opportunity to be in their College Program, I earned my "ears" of learning and living into incredible guest service. Being able to take those weekly marketing classes while at Walt Disney World was invaluable to my career. I always point with two fingers now and smile every time I see a hidden Mickey.

7. NBC Today Show.

The peacock makes me smile. It's the channel I stay on the longest when TV surfing and it's the only morning show I seem to connect to the hosts over the years when I get to watch a bit on a rare sick day.

8. USA Today.

I asked for a subscription for my 19th birthday in college. It's a paper that I always look at in the airport and I love to read it because of the snapshot it gives of everything across the country—and which was way before Twitter and Facebook.

9. Mel's Diner.

During a scary pregnancy, bedrest, NICU and daily walks with newborn twins—a nearby Mel's chocolate shake was my motivation, my reward and my normalcy. It's the best chocolate shake I ever had, but only comes close to those in junior high we used to have every day for lunch with french fries.

10. Armoire.

My favorite clothing rental website was born out of my favorite Seattle. They have the best customer service ever (Shefali!), as well as incredible deals and beautifully made clothes that I shriek with delight when I open up the package to see tags still on of a $200 value jacket I get to borrow for the week. If I had this service in my 20s and 30s, I no doubt would have received an increase in my confidence and in my paycheck.

LETTERS OF GRATITUDE

Dear Dad,

Thanks for letting me go through your mail at age 10 by sifting through the garbage bag on Sundays on the floor with you in the living room, which opened my eyes to your work, the bills, the University alumni magazines in the world outside. I will always be a Pepsi and Doritos fan thanks to those living room Sundays watching football with you and going through your garbage.

Thank you for letting me explore my interest in cooking, food, travel and people... from our own kitchen table. Do you still have the three ring binders and recipes that you paid me 50 cents each for recipes that I rewrote and your favorite ones to try? Of course, we never cooked them, but it sure kept me busy and quiet and curious and hungry.

Thank you for working hard and pursuing those once-in-a-lifetime opportunities in another state that enabled me to truly be set out on another path that would be my own. Being brave to say yes to move your family made me brave eventually and over time to meet new friends and try something new. Middle school and high school were hard enough without being the new, shy and quiet girl who tried all the sports and didn't excel in any. However, I learned to say yes and try because you did. The family dinners of Chinese food and ice cream while making the decision to move certainly didn't hurt either, and were great memories I will always have.

There are only a few times that I could, but wouldn't, remind you that I was right, that I proved you wrong and that sometimes I may have a better business sense than you. You may recall that the only birthday present I never got on my wish list was the $50 in stock for Starbucks IPO at $5 a share when I was a teenager. I thought it would be fun to follow the company on the stock market since I was there every day anyway. Don't worry, I don't know what it's worth now.

Thank you for letting me learn about business and leadership and people. Thank you for doing the right thing at work to build trust and respect, that perhaps unknown to you at the time, helped me decades later in Colorado to build relationships with the same people you encountered at work.

Dear Mom,

Thank you for being the heart of our family. You left your big family for a foreign state as a bride. You built a home and growing community of friends to call family decades later.

Thank you for the hundreds and hundreds of envelopes filled with notes and goodies that you have sent me over several decades. Thank you for filling the notes with your love...short notes, long letters, stamps, stickers, comics, news clippings, fashion tips, clothing catalogs, and of course candy, cookies, and more treats.

Thank you for teaching me to golf. I kicked and screamed my way there when we left a nice Saturday at home for a wet and cloudy nine holes to walk when I was younger, but at least we were guaranteed hot fries at the end of the round. The start of my career was hugely supported by my ability to join the guys on the golf course at tournaments and fundraisers. I could hold my own, hit it straight, know the etiquette and drink a beer. I learned that last one on my own.

Thank you for making every Christmas a special one for reconnecting with old and new friends, family and extended community across the country. The best part every year of my new year is receiving your box of the hundreds of Christmas cards you received and of course along with a few candy canes, so I could spend every night for a week reading about my fifth grade teacher's grandson, my aunt's remodeled kitchen, dad's college roommate's promotion in New York, and the picture of my kindergarten boyfriend and his beautiful family. I love that you have kept in touch with hundreds of people who have been in our lives and learn what others are doing and cheering them on from the distances.

Dear Matt,

Thank you for being my best friend. Thank you for thinking of our financial future together when we were just dating. Thank you for teaching me to prioritize life, not working weekends and to stop for a break. Thanks for teaching me tenacity, dedication, compassion, relentlessness and the power of being direct, honest and thoughtful with communications at work. Thank you for loving me, for putting up with me sharing my crazy fears, worries and conspiracy theories...and letting me share with you verbally so I could let it go. Thank you for planning your trips to create opportunities, for saying yes to new travel adventures and experiences for us before and after our family grew. Thank you. I love you.

Dear President G.W. Bush,

Thank you for raising two great daughters that while they have followed a few years behind me, they are proud daughters we can all look up to. Strong-willed and successful in our own right of jobs, love, careers, children and now grandparents that respect us too.

I've been able to be connected to you in one way or another in what seems relevant to milestones in my life.

When I was 10 years old, I was sitting

in front of you at a baseball game as you were about to become a baseball owner and I knew at the time you were the son of a President. I didn't at the time have too many idols except for Andre Agassi's poster on my wall, but it was my first encounter with someone famous and you seemed down to earth as you laughed and enjoyed the game.

When in my 20s, I was cheering for you on your first election night, hundreds of yards away from the Austin Capitol and only to wake up 12 hours later with no news of a President, was invited to attend an election fundraiser event in Denver with 500 friends in my first full-length gown, and then later was mailed a letter from your chief of staff recognizing my application for a job.

During your last year of office, I was able to be in DC to attend an event that you were at. I remember walking into the private 10x10 area within the reception hall where you and the First Lady greeted us one at a time. I finally formed the words to introduce myself, and meet you and your wonderful wife for sixty amazing seconds. After I embarrassingly stood on the wrong side of the First Lady and was reminded by you that pictures should always be "girl, boy, girl", you called after me as I was walking away to the horror of the Secret Service. You had remembered my company's name and wanted to share your appreciation for a tour you had recently received with the leadership and employees you had met. I again had to form words to thank you and agree to pass it on. Immediately after that moment, and thinking back to being 10-years-old, I was so grateful to realize that no matter how well known or powerful anyone is that we read about, regardless of beliefs, that we are all humans that can positively impact someone's life by how we simply treat each other and behave amongst strangers. Thank you for that, Mr. President.

Dear God,

Thank you for a wonderful day. Thank you for good food to eat, a warm bed to sleep in and a dry house to live in. Thank you for my wonderful family. I pray for my sibling(s), for my mommy and daddy, for my grandmas and grandpas, for all my aunts, uncles, cousins, friends, family, and teachers that love me so much. I pray that I have a good

night sleep all night long and I look forward
to a wonderful day tomorrow.

ACKNOWLEDGEMENTS

This amazing beautiful project was made possible by my crew of collaborators. Huge thanks and a debt of gratitude to my book coach Cynthia Gregory, who introduced me to my layout expert and publisher, Lilly Penhall. Also thanks to my friend and initial editor Sandy, to Brei for taking my calls on her vacation, and to Batol for the title brainstorm session. I've had this book in my mind and heart for more than a decade. When I shared my vision of this book this past year with my dear confidants Samantha Ballard and Leslie Field Young, only then did it seem real and achievable with their encouragement. When you decide to start a journey, bring all the friends you can find along with you to make it happen in a way that everyone can be proud to be a part of.

About Betsy Jean

Betsy is a country girl born in Montana and a West Coast city girl. Always interested in politics, she was a student government nerd and was also drawn to business at an early age. She had a successful lemonade stand and was a Girl Scout cookie top seller, which earned her a cool Walkman stereo. Betsy tried every sport without success except for varsity tennis and a hole-in-one at the age of sixteen. Betsy tried every internship in college and landed her first best job at the state Chamber of Commerce in Colorado. As a successful business and policy communicator for over twenty years, she still enjoys working with smart people at smart companies. Betsy currently enjoys visiting farmers markets in the San Francisco Bay Area with her family.

Do Good. Be Kind.
Foundation

Established in 2017, Do Good. Be Kind.®
is a movement that has reached around the
world inspiring people everywhere to take
action, to do more good, and to live with
kindness in mind.

In 2019, over 10,000 students in grades
K-12, took the Do Good. Be Kind.® pledge; a
promise to:

Be Accountable

Do Good

Be Kind to Myself

Be Kind to Others

Be Kind to the World Around Me

A portion of the purchase of this book will be donated to the Do Good. Be Kind. Foundation to help ensure that students in all schools will have access to this timeless message.

Learn more at dogoodbekind.org

More Books by Penhall Publishing

Fiction:

The Jenna Glynn Ghost Stories Series by Vicki Smart Penhall

Lies From the Past: A Viet Nam Tale by Vicki Smart Penhall

The Julian Joke by RT Shoemake

Poetry:

O, Poetry by Lilly Penhall and Photography by Rosie Lindsey

Strangely Wonderful by James Barrett Rodehaver

Bruises & Love Bites by Trier Ward

Sawdust, Soap, Soil & Stars by Lori Lasseter Hamilton

The Hollowscape by Trier Ward

Anthologies:

Not Dead Yet: An Anthology of Survivor Poetry

www.penhallpublishing.com

Made in the USA
Monee, IL
23 November 2021